COPYRIGHT

Numerology For Pets - A book on how to choose the right name for your pets and emphasize the good qualities in their behavior.

Cover and cartoons designed by Marcelo Mattos (Gordo)

Author: Hiezza Rosetti

Co-author: Giana Rosetti

Editor: Lynn LeGlaire

Published by Scriber Publishing Company

ISBN 978-0-9831949-1-0

Library of Congress Control Number: 2011901086

This book is also distributed in electronic format.

Version 1.0

Table of Contents

ACKNOWLEDGEMENT

To everyone who loves nature and animals.

To my daughters Giana and Gina, my grandson Giancarlo.

To my nephew Marcelo Mattos (Gordo) who gave my book a unique personality by designing its characters.

And a special acknowledgement to every pet that makes this world a better place to live.

"You get to know people's character by the way they treat animals".

PREFACE

After working for more than 20 years in numerology for people, and recommending the most appropriate names for babies, companies, artists, and several other professionals, I decided to analyze names for animals searching to identify their psychological profile.

I started with my own pets, whose names had been chosen randomly. I noticed that they did not have a very satisfactory numerological analysis. At the same time, my neighbors were asking me to suggest names for their pets.

I then got Uri, my dog. I wanted him to become a playful and a mellow dog. By doing his numerology, I got the characteristics I wanted: a mellow and playful animal.

I combined the two things that I love most: my profession and animals. Now, I can say that there are some differences between numerology for humans and for pets, and many times, the meanings are different as well.

By learning some techniques presented in this book, you will be able to emphasize good qualities in your pet's behavior by carefully selecting a name.

I hope to pass my knowledge on and increase the harmony between you and your pets.

Enjoy this book!

BASICS

ABOUT NUMEROLOGY

WHAT IS NUMEROLOGY?

Numerology is the study of the symbolism of numbers. It is used to determine a person or an animal's personality, strengths, talents, and obstacles to be overcome, including inner needs, emotional reactions, and ways of dealing with others.

The roots of numerology can be traced back 10,000 years to Egypt and Babylonia. Pythagoras, who developed many of the basic theorems that form the foundation of modern mathematics, is credited with formally organizing the field of numerology about 2600 years ago in ancient Greece.

HOW NUMEROLOGY WORKS?

Everything in the universe vibrates at its own particular frequency. By finding the vibration rate of any object, you can establish the qualities and energies associated with it. You can determine the major frequencies of different people by applying the principles of numerology, and using only the name and birth date as basic data.

This numerological analysis provides significant insight into people's personalities and their characters.

For pets, their natural temperament will count for 70% and the names chosen will count for 30%.

Story

A couple bought a Doberman puppy hoping that when he grew up he would guard the house, be alert to any strange noise, and be aggressive as well.

When he was little, the Doberman was mellow and played excessively. His owner still thought that he would be a beast once he grew up. The owner named the dog "Hoover", which is number THREE in numerology.

Well, Hoover kept playing even after he became an adult, and nothing would stop Hoover from playing. The owner kept saying to himself; "At least, his size will scare people away".

After some time, the same family received a little Fox Terrier as a gift. They named the dog Igor, which is number FOUR in numerology.

Igor was really smart, but he had an unpredictable temper and liked to bite everybody. Whenever the family arrived home, Hoover, the Doberman, would greet them, while Igor, the little dog, would bite Hoover. It was funny watching the big Doberman being bitten by that little Fox Terrier.

To prevent this type of situation, you should know how to choose the correct name for your pet. The numerology of a name will form the character of a person, a pet, a product or even a business.

NUMEROLOGY

How to Analyze a Name

The NAME of your pet has to be analyzed in three different ways:

1. Personality = It is the sum of all letters in the name. See *"Finding Your Pet's Personality"* on page 17.

2. Instinctive Reactions = It is the first vowel of their names. See *"Your Pet's Instinctive Reactions"* on page 29.

3. Inner Behavior = It is the sum of all vowels. See *"Discerning Your Pet's Inner Behavior"* on page 35.

Numerology for All Animals

Numerology works as follows:

- We visualize the name
- We speak the name
- We hear the name

In this process, we build up a sound that provokes a positive or negative reaction. Just like humans, animals create a psychological profile through hearing their names. It is like a note of a melody made through the letters that form the words. Each word has a sound, and each animal has a different hearing frequency.

The Basic Numerology Calculation

In the basic calculation in numerology, the numbers are reduced by simple addition.

In numerology for animals, all numbers are reduced to single digits, 1 through 9. The numbers 1, 2, 3, 4, 5, 6, 7, 8, and 9 represent the major vibration rates associated with animals' characteristics.

The number 15, for instance, is reduced by adding 1 + 5 to get 6. Correspondingly, the number 1974 can be reduced by adding 1 + 9 + 7 + 4 to get 21. The 21 can be further reduced by adding 2 + 1 to get 3.

The letters in a name are converted to numbers and then added together. These numbers, in turn, are also reduced.

The letter A, for instance, is 1; the letter B is 2; the letter C is 3, and so forth.

The table below shows the numbers assigned to the alphabet.

1	2	3	4	5	6	7	8	9
A	B	C	D	E	F	G	H	I
J	K	L	M	N	O	P	Q	R
S	T	U	V	W	X	Y	Z	

Learn to Add the Letters

Example 1: TATOO

1. Write down the name to be analyzed following the table above.

$$T = 2, \ A = 1, T = 2, O = 6, O = 6$$

2. Add the numbers and simplify them into ONE number.

TATOO = 2+1+2+6+6=17. The number 17 is equal 1+ 7=8.

Therefore, EIGHT is the number to be analyzed.

Example 2: SMOKY

1. Get the equivalent number for each letter from the table above:

$$S = 1, M = 4, O = 6, K = 2, Y = 7$$

2. Add the numbers and simplify them into ONE number:

$1 + 4 + 6 + 2 + 7 = 20$. The number 20 is equal $2 + 0 = 2$.

Therefore, TWO is the number to be analyzed.

Nick Names

Once you choose a name for your pet, avoid giving him a nick name. For instance, a dog can sense sounds at four times the distance that a human can. If you understand how your dog hears, you'll be able to communicate better with him because you'll see how he perceives the world.

Compared to humans, who can hear frequencies between 20 Hz and 20,000 Hz, dogs can hear sounds between 67 Hz and 45,000 to 60,000 Hz, depending on the breed.

Animals depend on their acute sense of hearing to survive, to hunt, to protect, to detect and to perform.

Story

John's kids were always asking him for a dog, but John always said no to his kids.

One day, John got home and saw his kids playing with this cute puppy. It was a gift from John's parents to his kids. John decided to keep the puppy and make his kids happy.

Well, it came the time to choose a name for the dog. Then the family got together and started brain storming on different names. Finally, they chose "Jefferson" as the name for the puppy, which is number EIGHT in numerology.

For few days, the kids, John and his wife called the puppy Jefferson, but then John started calling the puppy "Jeff"(number NINE), and his kids were calling the puppy "J" (number ONE).

Time passed and the dog started getting a little confused and sometimes ignoring the family when called. Jeff, the puppy, preferred spending his time playing with his own toys.

The family, not knowing what was going on with the dog, decided to take the dog to the veterinarian and have his ears checked. The veterinarian checked Jeff and found nothing wrong with him.

When the dog went back to the waiting room, the veterinarian heard the dog being called by many different names: "Is Jeff OK?" "Jefferson, come here baby!" "J, let's play!"

The veterinarian immediately realized that the dog was confused hearing so many names. He kindly advised the family to call the dog by one name only.

The family went back home and chose "Jeff" as the official name for the dog.

A few days later, Jeff, the dog, was answering everybody's call and playing with the kids.

So, when choosing a name for your pet, stick with it, and avoid calling your pet by a different name.

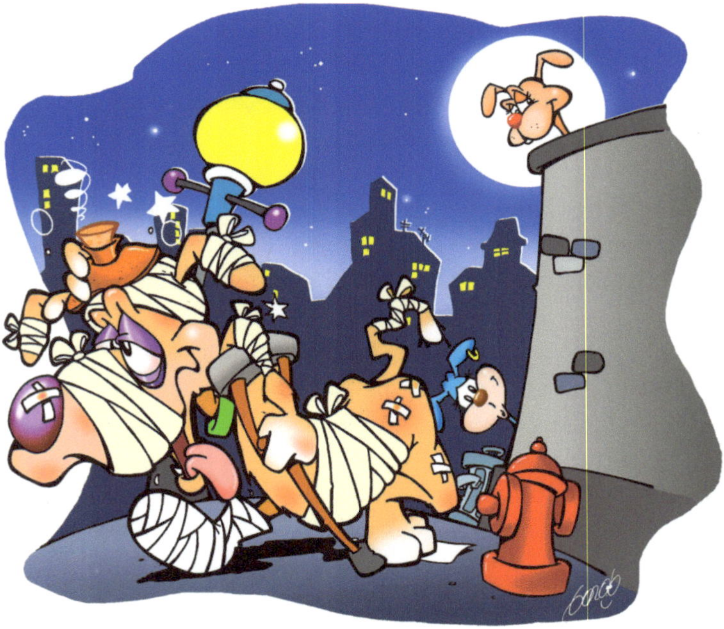

FINDING YOUR PET'S PERSONALITY

Add all letters of the name including consonants and vowels.

Example: Let's analyze the name Thunder

THUNDER

1	2	3	4	5	6	7	8	9
A	B	C	D	E	F	G	H	I
J	K	L	M	N	O	P	Q	R
S	T	U	V	W	X	Y	Z	

T + H + U + N + D + E + R = 2+8+3+5+4+5+9 = 36

36 = 3 + 6 = 9

Therefore, NINE is the number to be analyzed.

In the following pages you will find the meaning of each number and its correspondent personality characteristics.

NUMBER ONE

PERSONALITY

Number ONE pets are natural leaders but not good followers. They are active, independent, agile, love freedom, and may have a tendency to run away. They are emotionally unstable, anxious, and very intelligent. They can get depressed if their owners don't give them enough attention.

Number ONEs are also very persistent and have an excellent sense of smell. For females, the qualities and negative characteristics are enhanced. Avoid number ONE for cats, especially Siamese cats.

HEALTH

The number ONEs may have problems related to stress, nausea, fevers, digestive system, eyes, and teeth.

Example of number ONE names:

Plato, Rin Tin Tin, Flash, Jedi, Sabrina, Bono, and Aloha.

"The love that you give your pet is a thousand times repaid."

NUMBER TWO

PERSONALITY

Number TWO pets are anxious, nervous, loving, sociable, intuitive, lively, and people oriented. They are also stubborn, choosing one place to stay. They are territorial and like to leave their scent.

Both males and females have the ability to sense their owner's feelings or if any stranger represents danger. This number is excellent for animals that participate in shows, auctions, and competitions.

HEALTH

Number TWOs need to be exercised to prevent excessive fat and future cardiovascular problems. Special attention should be given to their jaws and mouth.

Example of number ONE names:

White, Rex, Jolly, Max, Wolf, Charlie, Oscar, Bingo, and Aria.

"Have a pet and you will know what unconditional love is."

NUMBER THREE

PERSONALITY

Number THREE pets are usually pretty, playful, friendly and intelligent. In training, they appear to be distracted and indifferent, but they will surprise you and perform for you when you least expect it. They also need constant stimulation and attention.

They are dependent on people, good guards, and love to be spoiled. Females are more extroverted than males. Do not lock them up or they will become very distressed.

HEALTH

Number THREEs have a tendency to have liver problems. They easily throw up. The youngsters may eat and chew everything they find around the house.

Examples of number THREE names:

James, Luna, Zac, Ben, Baby, Tabbie, Cissy, and Argus.

"The biggest coward is one who destroys nature."

NUMBER FOUR

PERSONALITY

Number FOUR pets are short tempered. If something out of the ordinary happens, their reactions can be unpredictable. This number is good for guard dogs, race horses or rodeo animals. They may get attached and obey one person only.

Usually, females are smarter than males, and show their feelings for people they dislike.

HEALTH

Their diet needs attention. Number FOUR animals need to be exercised daily. Their stomach is the fragile part of their bodies.

Examples of number FOUR names:

Roy, Ruth, Lord, Rambo, Daisy, Princess, Puff, Bell, and Buster.

"The wagging of a dog's tail and the purring of a cat are priceless."

NUMBER FIVE

PERSONALITY

Number FIVE pets are active, anxious, fast learners, loving, lively, and energetic. Number FIVEs don't like to be restrained. They love freedom and may become runaways.

They adapt easily to their new environment. They usually like people around them. Females are more curious and sociable than males.

HEALTH

Number FIVEs can be very active animal. They need exercise like walking, jumping, racing, etc. They are also subject to sudden fevers and cardiovascular problems.

Examples of number FIVE names:

Frank, Gigi, Joy, Tiger, Bella, Bristol, Califa, and Ataria.

"Dogs teach us how to love and be faithful."

NUMBER SIX

PERSONALITY

Number SIX pets are family oriented, jealous, and anxious. They are capable of eating everything they see around. The number SIXs are stubborn, docile, likeable, pretty, and attract the attention of everyone.

Females are more loving, better balanced, and calmer than males. Both genders may become insecure if they don't have affection or a serene environment.

HEALTH

Number SIX pets need a balanced nutrition. Avoid giving them too many treats. They tend to choose their own path to walk or play. SIXs may be subject to lymphatic problems.

Example of number SIX names:

Delta, Dino, Fred, Sam, Callie, Liona, Bali, Ginger, and Billy.

"Pets can decrease human depression and facilitate its cure."

NUMBER SEVEN

PERSONALITY

Number SEVEN pets are nice, friendly, observant, attentive, alert and usually tranquil. They like to dig holes and sometimes their behavior can be unpredictable if they don't get enough attention.

They are known to do foolish things such as urinating in places where they shouldn't. Females are generally more irritable than males. They usually choose a place to be alone.

HEALTH

Number SEVEN pets need a low calorie diet and they don't like rough exercises. Their bladder is the weakest part of their body.

Examples number of SEVEN names:

Quick, Jack, Dark, Foxy, Ania, Bliss, and Scooby.

"Respect nature because we are also animals."

NUMBER EIGHT

PERSONALITY

Number EIGHT pets are fast learners and good leaders. They are docile, sweet, jealous, and good guards. They show us affection, dynamism, and stubbornness.

Number EIGHT pets are easily trained because of their curiosity, and they do whatever it takes to get some treats. So, pay attention to what your pet likes. Females are mellower than males.

HEALTH

Number EIGHT pets need exercise to control their stress. Their back legs and joints are the fragile part in their body.

Examples of number EIGHT names:

Lobo, Ray, Zeus, Bacon, Ivory, Jasmine, and Snowball.

"Learn from your pet how to give yourself unconditionally."

NUMBER NINE

PERSONALITY

Number NINE pets are loving, friendly, docile and jealous. They need lots of love and they will generally follow one person.

They need attention, and will do whatever it takes to get it from you. They are anxious, intuitive, high spirited, and they hate being left alone. Females are generally needier than males.

HEALTH

Number NINE pets are prone to depression. Make sure you give your number NINE pet lots of love. They tend to have poor digestive systems.

Examples of number NINE names:

Half, Boris, Sparky, Holly, Jag, Coco, Sandy, and Avatar.

"Adopt a Snout!"

YOUR PET'S INSTINCTIVE REACTIONS

The analysis of the first vowel of your pet's name will describe its instinctive reactions.

Example: THUNDER

First Vowel = U = 3

The Value of the vowels:

A	E	I	O	U
1	5	9	6	3

Now, we have to know the meaning of each vowel as follows:

Vowel	Meaning of the First Vowel of a Name Instinctive Reactions
A	They are impulsive, independent, smart, active, anxious, outgoing, and alert.
E	They are intelligent, high spirited, lively, and have runaway tendencies. Sometimes they can be nervous, and usually very playful.
I	They are friendly, docile, devoted, loyal, affectionate, and need a harmonious environment to thrive. They don't like harsh words or yelling.
O	They are loving, jealous, active, easygoing nature, and fond of their family. Their home is their world.
U	They are joyful, very smart, sociable, graceful, guarding instincts, and children oriented.

Exceptions:

Names like Sylvia, the letter Y sounds like the vowel I. In this case, the first letter to be analyzed will be Y, which is number SEVEN. The same is true for any other name where the first letter sounds like a vowel. Don't forget that animals have a very acute sense of hearing.

BIRTHDAY

Here I will mention the date of birth just as a curiosity. It really doesn't have much weight in the animal's numerology. But if you know when your pet was born, you can use the calculation and the meanings of the numbers below. This may help you to get to know your pet better.

Example: August 3rd, 2009 or 8/3/2009

Do the following: $8 + 3 + 2 + 0 + 0 + 9 = 22 = 2 + 2 = 4$

The number 4 will be the number to be analyzed.

Number	Birth Characteristics
1	Your pet is independent, territorial, and a leader. He can be stubborn when learning new tricks. He doesn't like to be commanded.
2	Your pet is affectionate and needs your presence. He can be anxious and he is a fast learner.
3	Your pet likes to call attention to himself. He is very playful and docile. He likes hearing the human voice.
4	Your pet has a strong temper and he takes his time to learn new things. He doesn't like other animals around him and he can be very jealous.
5	Your pet is very active, fast learner, playful, adventurous, and independent. Sometimes he has a tendency to run away.
6	Your pet is family oriented and loves music. He is also loving and very stubborn.
7	Your pet is affectionate but cautious of others. He may choose his own place to stay alone.
8	Your pet is playful, and he can be a compulsive eater. He is very loving and strong willed.
9	Your pet doesn't like to be alone. If neglected he will do whatever he can to get your attention. He is also loving and friendly.

How to Harmonize Your Pet's Name

Basic rules:

In the previous chapters you learned how animals react when their chosen name is called. When getting a pet, try to learn as much as you can about his background, and his parents' personalities. Were the parents docile pets? Like humans, animals will take after their parents' temperament.

If it is not possible to research the background of your pets, then go by their race characteristics. In the following pages, I mention some dogs and cats breed characteristics. If your pet's breed is not listed, you can easily find it through an Internet search. The education you give to your pet will also influence his behavior.

If you just got your pet, the ideal situation would be to observe him for few days without naming him while studying his behavior. Determine if he is fearful, joyful, playful, etc. Observe what you like or don't like about his personality and then choose the name.

Choose a short name. Try to identify where the accent is on the name. Normally the emphasis is on the first vowel.

Listen to the sound of the name carefully because it will be the way your pet will hear it. Once the name is chosen, avoid giving your pet a nickname as he will most likely be confused by it.

If you feel that the name you have chosen is not a good name, you can choose another name. Don't forget to calculate the numbers before changing names and always pay attention to how your pet reacts to the sound of the chosen name.

DISCERNING YOUR PET'S INNER BEHAVIOR

The sum of all vowels represents your pet's inner behavior. This inner behavior is what they usually feel emotionally and express through their eyes, ears, and tails.

Characteristics of the total sum of the vowels:

Example: T H U N D E R

Vowels found: U and E - U = 3, E = 5

The total number for the vowels is 3 + 5 = 8

Now go to the next table and find the meaning of each number found when you have added all the vowels together.

Number	Meaning of the Total Sum of the Vowels Inner Behavior
1	Your pet is very curious and likes to explore everything around his territory. He likes to learn new things as well.
2	Your pet is well balanced. He is sensitive, nervous and likes his routine.
3	Your pet is intuitive, easily distracted, and adores children. He is very mellow.
4	Your pet likes affection, but sometimes doesn't know how to attract it. He can be very moody at times.
5	Your pet is impulsive and tame, and suddenly can do something unexpected. He is intelligent and likes to show you what he knows.
6	Your pet has a tendency to whine, and doesn't like to be alone. He can be very loving and stubborn at times.
7	Your pet is intuitive and likes affection. He needs to be respected when he wants to be alone.
8	Your pet is a natural leader and energetic. His behavior can change without warning. The best way to deal with the number EIGHT is to keep rewarding treats close to you.
9	Your pet is very loving, friendly, and likes to learn new tricks. Sometimes he chooses to be alone. He is also very independent.

THE IMPORTANCE OF THE BREED IN NUMEROLOGY

It is important to know your pet's breed temperament, so you can choose a name that will be pleasant to them. In this section, I mention the main characteristics of cat and dog breeds. If you don't find your pet's breed here, do an Internet search to know more about their temperament. It is important to know the following when choosing a breed:

- Aggression and protectiveness
- Energy, activity level, and playfulness
- Intelligence
- Loyalty
- Sensitivity
- Compatibility with other animals
- Behavior around children

BEHAVIOR OF SOME DOG BREEDS

AIRDALE TERRIER

Behavior – They are playful, friendly, loving, loyal, and totally trustworthy with children. They don't like to be alone and love digging holes wherever they can.

Numerology – Avoid the number 1 and 5 names, and first vowels "A", "E", and "U".

AKITA

Behavior – They need patience, love and kindness. Training should start early. Akitas are very loyal to their owners. Don't ever use brutality. It is important to socialize your Akita early with other dogs and people. They can jump very high.

Numerology – Avoid number 1, 4, 5, and 7 names, and "A" and "E" as first vowels.

BASSET HOUND

Behavior – For those who like dogs to sit quietly in a corner and just watch the world go by, this is the right breed. Bassets are hard to train, stubborn, and independent. They need their space.

Numerology – Due to their independence, it is best to avoid number 7 names. You may choose "O" as first vowel for their names.

BEAGLES

Behavior – They like people, animals and children. They need to be stimulated, otherwise, they will find something to destroy. They are stubborn and jealous.

Numerology – Avoid numbers 1 and 7 names, and first vowel "E".

BICHON FRISE

Behavior – This breed is smart, very loving, cheerful, and good companions. They don't like being harassed. These dogs are great for apartments, and they are very adaptable. Avoid spoiling them too much. They are fast learners and can be well trained.

Numerology – Avoid numbers 9 and 4 names, and first vowel "I".

BOSTON TERRIER

Behavior – Boston Terriers have strong and friendly personalities. They can range in temperaments from those that are eager to please their master to those that are more stubborn. They can be easily trained given a patient and assertive owner.

Numerology – Avoid number 1 and 5 names, and first vowels "A" and "E".

BOXER

Behavior – They are friendly and very playful. Their temperament is moderate in all respects. They are fast learners, but sometimes difficult to perform. Patience is needed to train them.

Numerology – Avoid number 4 names, and first vowel "A".

BULLDOG

Behavior – Bulldogs can be so attached to their family that they will not venture out of the yard without a human companion. They get along well with children, other dogs and pets. They are also very stubborn.

Numerology – Avoid number 9 names, and first vowel "E".

CHIHUAHUA

Behavior – They are territorial and protective. Chihuahuas can be easily provoked to attack, and are generally unsuitable for homes with small children. Chihuahuas crave attention, exercise, and love.

Numerology – Because of their personality, avoid number 1, 4 and 5 names, and first vowels "A" and "E".

COCKER SPANIEL

Behavior – This breed is generally even tempered, affectionate and gentle. They love to please their masters. They are the ultimate child's companion.

Numerology – Avoid number 1 and 4 names, and first vowel "A".

COLLIE

Behavior – This breed has qualities of loyalty, intelligence and gentleness. They are easily trained. Avoid scaring them when they are little as they can easily be traumatized for life.

Numerology – Avoid number 4 names, and first vowel "E".

DACHSHUND

Behavior – Dachshunds get along well with children and other pets. They are family dogs and cry a lot when left alone. They are stubborn, difficult to train, anxious, and demanding.

Numerology – Because of their anxiety, avoid numbers 1, 4, and 9 names, and first vowels "A" and "I".

DOBERMAN PINSCHER

Behavior – Doberman are loving, loyal, and alert watchdogs with

natural guarding qualities. They have quick reactions to anything. They can become hyperactive if deprived of exercise.

Numerology – Avoid number 4 names, and first vowel "A."

FOX TERRIER

Behavior – They are extremely energetic, but not suitable for families with other pets. They are intelligent but sometimes difficult to train.

Numerology – Because they tend to run away, avoid number 1, 4, and 5 names, and first vowels "A" and "E" as well.

GERMAN SHEPHERD

Behavior – The intelligence of this breed is legendary. They want to please and are sensitive to the moods of their owners. They have protective instincts and love children. They are easily trained.

Numerology – Avoid number 1, 4, and 7 names, and first vowel "A".

GOLDEN RETRIEVER

Behavior – Golden Retrievers are calm, naturally intelligent and obedient. They are very intuitive, family oriented, and one of the brightest dogs ranked by obedience command trainability.

Numerology – There are no restrictions numbers or first vowels for this breed.

HUSKIES

Behavior – They are loyal to their masters, intelligent, and stubborn. They need to be exercised and hate being left alone. Huskies are very intelligent and trainable, but they will only obey a command if

they see the human is stronger minded than themselves.

Numerology – Avoid number 1, 4, and 5 names, and first vowels "A" and "E".

LABRADOR RETRIEVER

Behavior – Labs are non aggressive towards people and great playmates for kids. Labs have a very long puppy phase, and can be terrible chewers during this time. They hate being left alone.

Numerology – Avoid number 9 names, and first vowel "I".

MALTESE

Behavior – Maltese are docile, loyal, devoted, smart, and easily trained. Maltese also suffer from separation anxiety, so potential owners should be aware of this behavior.

Numerology – Avoid number 7 and 9 names, and first vowel "I":

MINIATURE PINSCHER

Behavior – They are intelligent, lively, alert, and high-spirited with a unique personality. They can be aggressive and must have room to exercise or will become hyperactive. They are noisy and good with children.

Numerology – Because of their personality, avoid number 1, 4, and 5 names, and first vowels "A" and "E".

PITBULL

Behavior – They are intelligent, courageous, and obedient. They defend their family, and nothing intimidates them. Pitbulls are playful, and need to socialize with people and other animals.

Numerology – Avoid number 1 and 4 names, and the first vowel "A".

POODLE

Behavior – Poodles are intelligent, happy, lively, playful, easily trained, friendly, and outgoing. They are an excellent family dog for those who are prepared to maintain their grooming needs. Avoid leaving them alone.

Numerology – Avoid number 2, 6, and 9 names, and first vowels "A" and "I".

PUGS

Behavior – They are strong willed but rarely aggressive and suitable for families with children. They can be quiet and docile but also vivacious depending on their owner's mood.

Numerology – Avoid number 7 and 9 names, and first vowel "I".

ROTTWEILER

Behavior – This breed is intelligent, obedient and has guarding instincts. Trustworthy around children if raised with them. They need to be trained when they are still young.

Numerology – To prevent aggression, avoid number 1 and 4 names, and first vowel "A".

SCHNAUZER

Behavior – They are playful, active, alert, good guard, and companion. They are good with children if respected. They are easily trained and love to chase cats and other animals.

Numerology – Avoid number 1, 4, and 6 names, as well as first vowels "A", and "O".

WEST HIGHLAND TERRIER

Behavior – They are courageous, agitated, and determined. They love their owners and are easily trained. They need to be exercised regularly.

Numerology – Avoid number 1 and 5 names, and first vowels "A", and "E".

WEIMARANER

Behavior – These dogs are very protective of their family and can be very territorial. They need to be thoroughly socialized when young to prevent aggression. They are also highly intelligent and problem-solving animals, which earned them the epithet "dog with a human brain".

Numerology – Avoid the number 5 names, and first vowel "E".

YORKSHIRE

Behavior – This breed is sweet, delicate, affectionate, and the ultimate lap dog. They love to be pampered. They are intelligent and will do anything to please their owners. Good watchdogs despite their size.

Numerology – Avoid number 4 names, and first vowel "A".

MIXED BREEDS

Behavior – Usually, it's hard to know their breeds, unless you know their parents. Any mixed breed dog is an excellent dog. They are

usually very grateful to their owners, and do everything to please them. They can be wonderful guard dogs and defend their territory well. When trained, they learn new tricks fast.

Numerology – When getting a mixed breed, observe their reactions and behavior for some time, and then you can choose a name for your pet. As a tip, avoid number 4. No restrictions for first vowels.

BEHAVIOR OF SOME CAT BREEDS

ABYSSINIAN

Behavior – They are alert, active, intelligent, independent, easy to settle, and people oriented. Abyssinians are excellent at training people to do just what they want them to do.

Numerology – No restrictions.

BENGAL

Behavior – They are intelligent, friendly, assertive, and active. Some like to retrieve objects, and many like to climb and play in water. Their voices are sometimes rather wild-sounding.

Numerology – Avoid number 2 and 9 names, and first vowel "I".

BIRMAN

Behavior – Birmans are very intelligent and curious. They like to know what you are doing or about anything that is new. Birmans are people-oriented cats and don't like to be left alone. If not given enough love they will get your attention with a gentle love bite, just to tell you they are in need of you.

Numerology – Avoid number 7 and 9 names, and first vowel "I".

BURMESE

Behavior – They are the ideal lap cats. They are also playful, smart, good with children and other animals. Females are generally more demanding than males.

Numerology – No restrictions.

CORNISH REX

Behavior – They are playful, affectionate, fun and loving companions that enjoy being part of a busy household. They are also very acrobatic.

Numerology – Avoid number 2 and 9 names, and first vowel "I".

EGYPTIAN MAU

Behavior – Egyptian Maus are playful, busy, and sociable, as well as intelligent, independent, easy to settle, and people oriented.

Numerology – Avoid number 2, 9, and 7 names, and first vowel "I".

HIMALAYAN

Behavior – They are gentle, docile and cope quite well with

children and other animals. Himalayans are, for the most part, quiet creatures.

Numerology – Avoid number 7 and 9 names, and first vowel "I".

MAINE COON'S

Behavior – Easygoing nature makes this cat a fine companion for children and other pets. They are gentle, affectionate, and playful. They are also good mousers and like to retrieve objects.

Numerology – No restrictions.

PERSIANS

Behavior – They are gentle, quiet, and sweet-natured, Persians will not necessarily play with the kids. They prefer an atmosphere of serenity and security.

Numerology – Avoid number 7 and 9 names, and first vowel "I".

SCOTTISH FOLD

Behavior – Scottish Folds tend to become very attached to their owners and are very affectionate. They are playful, intelligent, loyal, soft spoken, and adaptable to home situations and people.

Numerology – No restrictions.

SIAMESE

Behavior – This popular breed is loyal, energetic, intelligent, sociable, affectionate, and tend to follow their chosen humans around the home. They are excellent with kids and generally dominate other cats in the household.

Numerology – Avoid numbers 2 and 9, and first vowel "I".

TONQUINESE

Behavior – They are very smart cats, faithful, and loyal to their owners. They love to talk and believe in feline's right to free speech. The Tonkinese craves affection and companionship.

Numerology – Avoid numbers 2 and 9 names, and first vowel "I".

TURKISH ANGORAS

Behavior – Angoras are graceful, playful, affectionate, loyal, and gentle. Angoras are also extremely busy, always on the move. These resourceful cats will invent their own toys if none are provided.

Numerology – No restrictions.

OTHER ANIMALS

BOVINES

For Auction and Shows – Use number 2 and 5 names. Also, try to pick "E" as first vowel.

For Rodeos – Number 4 is best for names.

Milk Cows – Choose number 6 names and "A" as the first vowel.

HORSES

For Auction and Shows – The number 2 is the best for names.

Races Horses – Choose numbers 1, 2, and 5 names, and "E" as first vowel. These numbers will give strength and speed to the horse.

Obstacle Course Horses – Avoid number 4 because it will make your horse very stubborn.

Rodeo Horses – Choose number 1 or 4 names, and "A" as first vowel.

GOATS

Behavior – They are agile and playful when small. They usually get attached to their caregivers. Goats are difficult to control. When they want something, they don't give up until they get it. They can be moody at times.

Numerology – Avoid number 1, 4, and 5 names, and first vowels "A" and "E".

Story

Lord was a white goat with brown spots. He was friendly and playful.

Because he was so cute, he was adopted by a farmer as a pet. Eventually he turned into the king of the house. His name was chosen for his imposing size. Everybody used to say: "He looks like a Lord."

The name Lord stuck, which is number four "FOUR", and has the letter "O" as its first vowel.

Lord grew up and became a big goat. He was strong, courageous, tough and moody. Nobody could go to the backyard without running from Lord, and if people weren't careful, Lord would butt them with his head. It was difficult for the farmer's family to deal with him.

The only way to prevent his aggression was to gain his respect by going to the backyard with some treats or a red flag tied to a stick.

One day, the farmer decided to buy a dog. Lord became friends with

the dog and stopped being aggressive towards people. What Lord really needed was a friend. Take a look at the meaning of number FOUR and first vowel "O".

SHEEP

Behavior – Sheep are sweet, easygoing, and easily taught. Often jealous, they tend to fight for their space.

Numerology – Avoid number 6 and 9 names, and first vowel "O".

RABBITS

Behavior – Rabbits are docile, playful, easily trained. They love affection and tend to seek the owner's lap. They like to dig holes and disappear if left alone in any garden. They are also very curious.

Numerology – Avoid number 1 and 5 names, and first vowels "A" and "E".

PIGS

Behavior – They bond quickly to humans and love to be close to their favorite people. Pigs have a gentle disposition and also love to play with toys.

Numerology – Avoid number 1 and 5 names, and first vowels "A" and "E".

Story

A newborn piglet was orphaned. Nobody wanted her and she was thrown into the garbage.

The piglet cried a lot in an attempt to draw attention from passersby.

Mary, who loved animals, passed by the garbage can and heard the baby pig crying. She got that little pink thing, and immediately the baby pig tried to suckle her fingers thinking it was food.

Mary took her home, gave the baby pig a bottle, and called her Rose, which is number THREE "3".

Mary raised Rose as her own baby, and Rose used to follow Mary everywhere. Rose always wore a ribbon around her neck calling attention to herself wherever she went. Very docile, always accompanying anyone who would give her something to eat.

Rose grew up, and was spayed. She had a strong appetite and started to gain weight. If Mary was not careful, Rose would steal food from visitors and even candies from children in the street. It was a common thing for Mary to hear from others; "Hum! This pig will make a great barbecue, sausage, or ham."

Mary was afraid for Rose. After all, Rose was very docile and easy to be taken. One day a man made an offer to Mary to purchase Rose, which was promptly refused.

The ideal day for Rose was to roll in the mud.

As a precaution, Mary limited Rose's time in the garden and would keep a careful eye on Rose fearing that someone might steal her.

The same man, who made Mary the offer, came with another offer.

This time, the man asked Mary if she would like to have Rose do some advertising and be a mascot for a soccer team.

Mary got very happy with the man's proposal and her beloved Rose became a star. Rose always received a big applause from the crowd while parading on the soccer field on a match day.

The soccer team had their uniform and so did Rose. She wore a big ribbon around her neck matching the colors of the soccer team's uniform.

Mary made lots of money, and Rose got to enjoy her life in a huge garden surrounded by bodyguards, while Mary proudly rested.

In this case, the number "THREE" and the first vowel "O" was the right numerological combination.

FERRETS

Behavior – Ferrets are nocturnal, often restless, and messy. They are also affectionate, caring, and correspond well to good treatment. Training should be done with calm and patience.

Numerology – Avoid number 1, 4, and 5 names, and first vowel "A" and "E".

Story

During a visit to a pet shop, a family felt in love watching a couple of ferrets sleeping in a hammock. The family asked the sales person questions about ferrets and their behavior.

They quickly learned that ferrets are nocturnal, and that they would

not leave their spacious cage.

The sales person said that ferrets were not high maintenance pets. The father thought: "What a relief!" If they were dogs, they would chew on everything". The family decided to buy the two ferrets.

They named the female Pink (number FIVE), and the male Greg (number ONE).

After a few days, the children persuaded their parents to allow the ferrets to play outside the cage in their closed bedroom to avoid the ferrets' escaping. So, Greg and Pink played freely and got used to sitting on the lap of everyone. It was an enjoyable time for the family.

One day, the family had a party to go to and they decided to leave the ferrets outside of their cage. They left the two ferrets to enjoy their free space.

What a surprise when they arrived from the party! Parts of the bedroom doors and closet were gnawed. Everything was stirred and out of place, and worse, nobody could locate the ferrets.

What a mess! Everybody called the ferrets out loud, but nothing happened. The children were crying for the loss of their pets.

Hours later, the family heard something falling from the kitchen cabinet. They rushed to the kitchen, and there they were, Pink and Greg eating whatever food they found available.

Well, needless to say that after that day, Pink and Greg were never

let loose without supervision.

Would a better choice of names make a difference? Probably! Remember that the animal natural temperament counts 70% and the names chosen count 30%.

So, before choosing a name for your pets, research their genetics and behavior.

SQUIRRELS

Behavior – They are playful, loving, and have a strong temper. They have a tendency to run away.

Numerology – Avoid number 1 and 5 names, and first vowels "A" and "E".

RACCOONS

Behavior – Raccoons live well with humans. They are very stubborn, independent, curious, and hard to train. They also have a great sense of smell and are very intelligent.

Numerology – Avoid number 4 and 5 names, and first vowels "A" and "E".

OPOSSUMS

Behavior – They can be good companions but hard to be domesticated. Males are more independent than females. Do not trust opossums around other pets unless they are used to them.

Numerology – Avoid number 4 names, and first vowel "E".

BIRDS

CANARIES

Behavior – Canaries are generally docile, and usually recognize those who feed them. If trained well, they can be let loose in the house and eat from people's hands.

Numerology –To prevent any escaping, avoid number 1 names and first vowel "A".

CHICKENS

Behavior – They are difficult to train. They can be docile and respond well if you show them food.

Numerology -The number 6 names and first vowel "O" may make them greedier.

GEESE

Behavior – When raised with love, they respond accordingly, otherwise they become aggressive. They are very intelligent and

wonderful guards.

Numerology – Avoid number 4 names, and first vowel "E".

Story

Mr. Smith bought a small ranch with a lake. To complete the landscape, he bought some ducks and few goslings who happened to be orphans.

He got a box, a suitable heater and started taking care of the little ones. Among them, there was a very small gosling that Mr. Smith thought it would not survive. He named the gosling Oswald (number TWO).

Every day, Mr. Smith used to walk around the ranch and the goslings followed him everywhere. Mr. Smith always carried Oswald in his arms because Oswald was too little.

The goslings grew up healthy and strong. They were not friendly with strangers, but very docile with the family.

Oswald grew up and became very attached to Mr. Smith. Every time Mr. Smith returned home, he called Oswald, and Oswald always came to greet Mr. Smith with open wings.

Oswald used to jump on Mr. Smith's shoulder and give him goose kisses. His behavior always touched Mr. Smith with happiness making him think: "How beautiful! He recognizes me!" Oswald became Mr. Smith's best friend and he could always count on Oswald's devotion and protection.

Now, review the qualities of number 2 and first vowel "O".

MACAWS

Behavior – Macaws are playful, active, and have a strong personality. This makes them a very challenging pet. They are also very affectionate, and in return require a good deal of time and attention from their owners to be happy. Macaws are very intelligent.

Numerology – Avoid number 1, 4, and 5 names, and first vowels "A" and "E".

PARROTS

Behavior – Parrots are very intelligent and intuitive as well as sensitive and jealous. They usually become attached to one person only.

Numerology – Avoid number 1, 4, and 6 names, and first vowels "A", and "O".

ASTROLOGY

In order to have an accurate astrological chart of your pet, it is necessary to know the exact time of birth, date, and place where he was born. Since most of us don't have this data for our pets, I will quickly mention characteristics of the astrological signs applicable to pets.

ARIES – March 21 to April 20

Behavior – Aries pets are generally anxious, nervous, and love biting everything they see. They are good runners and need exercise.

Health – They are prone to sudden fever, ear and teeth problems.

Numerology – Avoid number 1 names and first vowel "A".

TAURUS – April 21 to May 21

Behavior – Taurus pets love to eat anything they find lying around. They need to exercise to prevent overweight. They also like to

watch what is going on around them.

Health – They may have problems chewing, including throat and ear infections.

Numerology – If you want a tranquil animal choose number 2 names and first vowel "O".

GEMINI – May 22 to June 21

Behavior – Gemini pets are very active, energetic, playful, good eaters, and great hunters. They socialize very easily with humans and other pets.

Health – They may have problems in their legs.

Numerology – Avoid number 1 and 5 names, and first vowels "A" and "E".

CANCER – June 22 to July 23

Behavior – Cancer pets are family oriented and joyful. If mistreated, they will react with sadness. They hate being left alone.

Health – Problems with their stomach is common. They may vomit if food is not well digested.

Numerology – In order to decrease the Cancer pets' moodiness, avoid choosing number 4 names, and first vowel "I".

LEO – July 24 to August 23

Behavior – Leo pets love compliments, massages, and all the pampering you can give them. They love attention.

Health – Avoid putting these pets under stress and anxiety.

Numerology – Avoid number 1 and 5 names, and first vowels "A" and "E".

VIRGO – August 24 to September 21

Behavior – Virgo pets like to serve their master and perform tasks. They can be bored easily and need to be petted to increase their trust.

Health – Intestinal problems and subject to worms.

Numerology – Avoid number 4 names, and first vowel "A".

LIBRA – September 22 to October 23

Behavior – Libra pets are people oriented. They are usually mellow pets and like to be petted. They are playful and hate being alone.

Health – Always take care of their nutrition and make sure that they drink enough water.

Numerology – Choose number 2 names, and first vowels "U" and "O" to reinforce all good qualities of your Libra pet.

SCORPIO – October 24 to November 23

Behavior – Scorpion pets are beautiful and usually have a nice coat. Dogs like to play with water. Scorpion pets can be jealous.

Health – They are subject to skin allergies, so beware of perfumes and soaps. They are also sensitive to strong smells.

Numerology – Choose number 7 and 9 names, and first vowel "I".

SAGITTARIUS – November 24 to December 22

Behavior – These pets are beautiful, friendly, joyful, playful, and

love to walk. Sagittarius pets are fast learners.

Health – They are subject to circulatory and hip problems.

Numerology – Seek names ending in number 3, 5, and 8 names, and first vowels "U" and "O".

CAPRICORN – December 23 to January 21

Behavior – Capricorn pets are stubborn and moody at times. They don't like to be bothered. They usually get attached to one person.

Health – They subject to joint problems.

Numerology – Seek number 2, 3, and 5 names, and first vowel "A", "E", and "I".

AQUARIUS – January 22 to February 19

Behavior – The Aquarius pets are dynamic, sociable and playful. They need to be with people.

Health – They are subject to circulatory, spine, and thigh problems.

Numerology – Choose number 3 and 5 names, and first vowels "E" and "U".

PISCES – February 20 to March 20

Behavior – The Pisces pets have changeable moods. They can be good companions, but don't like many people around them.

Health – They may be subject to problems in their paws, lymphatic system or be sensitive to drugs.

Numerology – Avoid number 2, 4 and 9 names, and first vowel "A", "E", and "I".

SUMMARY

Here is the summary on how to choose a name for your pet.

Example: OREO

1- PERSONALITY: Sum of all letter of the name.

O = 6, R = 9, E = 5, O = 6   6 + 9 + 5 + 6 = 26   26 = 2 + 6 = 8

Meaning of Number EIGHT– Number EIGHT pets are fast learners and good leaders. They are docile, sweet, and jealous. They are also easily trained because of their curiosity, and they do whatever it takes to get some treats. So, pay attention to what your pet likes. Females are mellower than males.

2- REACTIONS – Look for the first vowel of the name, which is the letter O, and O is number SIX.

Meaning of Letter O – Loving, jealous, active, easygoing nature, and fond of their family. Their home is their world.

3- BEHAVIOR – Sum of all vowels of the name.

OREO = 6 + 5 + 6 = 17 which is number EIGHT.

Meaning: Your pet is a natural leader and energetic.

His behavior can change without warning. The best way to deal with the number EIGHT is to keep rewarding treats close to you.

Remember the Following:

1. The animal's natural temperament will count for 70% and the names chosen will count for 30%.

2. Avoid giving your pet a nick name, or call him by his name and nick name. He may get confused.

3. Watch your pet's behavior before giving him a name. Try to call him by a name you like and see how he reacts to each sound.

4. Try to know your pet's breed. If he is a mixed breed, try to see what the predominant breed is. It may help you to predict your pet's temperament, and it will be easier to choose a proper name for him.

5. Have fun with your pet!

EPILOG

Getting a pet is a life long commitment. The fact that you love your pet doesn't make you a good owner. They require, love, care, space, and proper nutrition. Sometimes, pets are more demanding than children.

On the other hand, having a pet will make you a happier human being. A pet will give you constant emotional fulfillment and unconditional love and acceptance.

They are always there for us, great listeners and they never judge us! At the end, we learn a lot from them.

Use this book as much as you can to select the perfect name for your pet. Every pet deserves our devoted attention.

HIEZZA ROSSETTI

A heart beats in all of us

ABOUT THE AUTHOR

Hiezza Rossetti is originally from Brazil. She has more than 30 years experience in astrology, numerology, graphology, tarot cards, and crystals.

She has appeared as a guest on various TV programs ranging from daytime to prime time shows to talk about her fields of expertise.

She also wrote many articles for various Brazilian magazines and newspapers on numerology and other esoteric topics.

Some of her most famous publications include the books "Color for Success" and "Numerology for Business".

Hiezza Rossetti lives in São Paulo, Brazil, where she is still very active in animal rights and esoteric studies.

www.ingramcontent.com/pod-product-compliance
Lightning Source LLC
Chambersburg PA
CBHW041221270326

41933CB00001B/1